# WORDS
## at the Fault-line of
# Faith
### and
# Science

J. D. Chapman

WESTBOW
PRESS®
A DIVISION OF THOMAS NELSON
& ZONDERVAN

WestBow Press books may be ordered through booksellers or by contacting:

WestBow Press
A Division of Thomas Nelson & Zondervan
1663 Liberty Drive
Bloomington, IN 47403
www.westbowpress.com
1 (866) 928-1240

ISBN: 978-1-5127-5789-7 (sc)
ISBN: 978-1-5127-5791-0 (hc)
ISBN: 978-1-5127-5790-3 (e)

Library of Congress Control Number: 2016915860

Print information available on the last page.

WestBow Press rev. date: 9/29/2016

One of the most verifiable writings from the first century is the letter composed by St. Paul to the members of the Church at Colossae, in what is now Turkey.
He writes, "He (Jesus Christ) is the image of the invisible God, the firstborn over all creation. For by Him all things were created, things in heaven and on earth, visible and invisible, whether thrones or powers or rulers or authorities; all things were created by Him and for Him. He is before all things and in Him all things hold together." NIV

This book is dedicated to my wife, Beverley, who has put up with me for almost thirty years, puts strange topics in my mind for musing and always corrects my syntax and spelling, whether the writings are science or poetry. She is one of the brightest lights of my life.

# TABLE OF CONTENTS

## STORIES JESUS TOLD AND GODLY COMMUNICATIONS....... 43

# INTRODUCTION

Words are the building blocks for communication between intelligent persons. With every language, people have somehow come together to agree on the meaning(s) of specific vocal and calligraphic expressions and those meanings are often known by the context in which they are spoken or written. And as I have come to learn, some languages contain multiple words that define different meanings whereas in English there is sometimes only one word for all the meanings. The use of words (language) is therefore a very deep and philosophical exercise that demands much more of our attention than it usually receives. The flippant use of language defines much of our comedy routines and humor, but it is good to laugh. Nevertheless, if we desire to better understand our world and our place in it, our rationalizations should be based in words whose meanings are precise. Such discourse continues to lead to a deeper understanding of the ways of mankind.

Why a research scientist trained in nuclear engineering and biophysics should attempt to put into words his deepest understanding of the physical world and his faith seems unusual. But throughout my career I have attempted to communicate through "everyday language" my thoughts at this exciting interface. I have been given the faith to believe in a God, a master creator, of all the physical world known to humankind today. You can be sure that there will be more discoveries and definitions to come. We creatures have been made with the capacity to inquire and understand. I do not have enough faith to believe that what we see, hear and feel are simply the transient expressions of different energy states of physical matter that are ever moving to greater heights of entropy. And so like many others, I have come to believe that my life has a meaning within this complex cosmic sea in which I find myself.

My educational training has taken me deep inside the molecular and atomic nature of physical matter and I have devoted my research career to devising improved ways for more efficiently killing those "outlaw" cells in human tumors that are treated with ionizing radiations to produce cancer cures. The fields of cell biology and biophysics have formed the basis of over two hundred contributions that my research contributed to the peer-reviewed literature. That research informed about the molecular mechanisms that produce cell killing by radiation and identified some novel means that could lead to improved treatments. I always spoke authoritatively about photons and electrons as if I had seen them or knew how to corral them but, in fact, laboratory research requires an enormous amount of faith in the science that has gone before. It is not possible for anyone to see photons or electrons but their effects can be measured by physical devices and biological systems. While directing laboratory research that qualified for competitive funding was exhilarating, the teaching of radiation mechanisms to graduate students and medical residents who would apply this knowledge to patients has brought me the greatest joy. The medical physics textbook, RADIOTHERAPY TREATMENT PLANNING –LINEAR/ QUADRATIC RADIOBIOLOGY, published in 2015 by CRC press was largely a summary of my laboratory efforts. To watch eager students of the basic sciences and those in training for clinical positions succeed in their careers has been most satisfying. But what does it all mean other than some personal gratification for me and my students.

So as a hobby throughout my research career I have resorted to finding the most informative words possible to describe most of my deepest questions. I have composed over five hundred poems in both rhyme and free verse to challenge my thinking on several matters. This has been a very private and personal habit but some of those poems have been of benefit to family and colleagues. Seventy-eight were assembled and published by Durango Publishing Corp. in a volume entitled, FAITH IN WORDS, in 2006. That grouping included some that were philosophical and some that were comic rhyme (my favorite) and was distributed to mainly family and close friends. Since that time, several additional poems have been composed that address the meaning of life in the context of the Christian faith. In retirement as one who has confronted the realities of aging and death on several fronts, the questions of "Who am I and why?" require some answers. The meaning of man's passage through the space-time domain in which we find ourselves and live is undoubtedly complex but demands some attention, especially if our understanding is to include a God.

In this volume, these new expressions of my best description of the physical world and how it relates to the teachings of Christ are presented along with some that were previously published in FAITH IN WORDS. Our knowledge about sub-atomic particles, our massive expanding universe and the molecular and biophysical basis of life forms is rapidly expanding. And it is within this milieu that Don Chapman finds himself relating to his wife, his children, his students, his colleagues and his neighbors through mechanisms of interaction that are not well defined nor verifiable by the laws of physics. So he has accepted the need for a God. And fortunately the Triune God of the Christian faith made himself (herself if you prefer) known when he took on all the anthropomorphic limitations of His created beings by becoming a human and communicating the meaning of life to His creatures. So I continue to read about one new book each week by authors who are also searching for meaning to their lives. These books range in genre from novels, history, sociology, theology and hard science. But my favorite read is that of poetry written by individuals who are also reaching out for meaning to their life in their unique words. Poetry for me is not an exercise in producing flowery and exotic words which show that I have great skills in English. Far from that, it is an exercise to place into words my deepest thoughts that can be understood and appreciated by my colleagues and friends. Some have called my rhyme and free verse "terse" and if that means it is succinct and to the point then I accept that classification as a complement. If it informs readers and prompts deep thoughts within them about the meaning of their life, it has fulfilled my objectives. And precise meanings for specific words is most important for excellence in communication. But I will add again, that poetry is a very personal expression of individual thinking and mine has been performed as a hobby to justify my rationalizations at the interface of faith and science.

A divergence between the physical/biological sciences and theology has occurred over the past one hundred or more years. Both studies attempt to define the meaning of human life in the context of its physical environment and the sciences have made major strides over that time. Our current understanding of the atomic makeup of matter is amazing and each additional year we learn of new bits that can exist in very expensive experimental devices for extremely brief times. At the other end of the dimension scale we have learned just how large the universe might be, how many years it has been in the making and the billions upon billions of stars with associated planets that can be detected by our costly observatories. Such vastness staggers the mind. In the space/time dimensions of human existence we have learned of the cellular makeup of we persons, about the master code (DNA) that contains all the information necessary for cellular differences and specialization and in some cases how these processes can go awry to produce unwanted disease. It's no wonder that many scientists have given up on any theological meaning to their deliberations. Some scientists don't need a God and believe that a Theory of Everything (TOE) will soon define all that can be known about human beings.

Theology, on the other hand, does not operate by the rules of scientific discovery and method but can provide a superior understanding of why humans experience joy, pain, love and a desire for community. I have described this divide in reasoning as a "fault-line" in that the advances that take place on one side are often not viewed as truth by the other. And the Christian Church has been negligent in many respects by reverting into a comfortable space where scientific facts have been disbelieved or trivialized. In fact, the field of philosophy (science + theology) which flourished for much of man's lifetime has been severed into competing factions which rarely get together to share their discoveries. It's not quite plate tectonics but these underlying forces have formed a rugged gap on the surface of academic discourse about what constitutes physical matter and how it got into the configurations where it can think and create. Some geologists teach that if the subterranean tension which produces the fault-line can be diminished, the surface gap which keeps the tectonic plates apart might shrink in size. Such an event could be very catastrophic. In spite of my broad reading in the areas of faith and science, I still have many doubts and questions that may never be fully resolved but that does not stop me from trying to bridge this gap. And having reviewed most of the theological thinking that is currently out there, I am confident that the Judeo/Christian understanding is the best available. Having been brought up in a strict Christian home has probably produced a bias in my thinking. What is unique to the Christian faith is the acceptance that Jesus Christ was the promised Jewish Messiah who entered the time and space of His creation to speak to humans with words that were from and about God. Those words that are printed in red color in some Bibles are a good place to start one's search for truth. So language and words have been and are still today the basis of Godly communications with mankind and words are very important to me as a scientist and amateur theologian. When we articulate descriptions of physical matter and personal sensing with precision, scholars are well on their way to know the how and why of human beings. If all the Doctors of Philosophy (Ph.D.) around the world would make time for defining who humans are and what they should be about, the fault-line could become smaller. Whose fault is it, anyway?

This collection of my thoughts in rhyme and free verse has been helpful for me to arrive at an understanding of who I am and what I should and can do with my life. If they encourage others to engage more deeply in their own discovery of their being and its surrounding world, these literary efforts will have succeeded.

The poems of this volume have been grouped into four sections that have been labeled WHO AM I AND HOW IT ALL HAPPENED (13), THE INVASION OF GOD INTO HIS CREATION (17), STORIES JESUS TOLD AND GODLY COMMUNICATIONS (22) and BLENDING SCIENTIFIC DISCOVERY AND FAITH (23). Some were published in the volume FAITH IN WORDS (2006) and are reprinted with permission of the author. The year of composition is included at the bottom of each poem to give some indication as to when they were chronologically created. They contain many repetitive (and sometimes monotonous) themes which obviously have been important to the author over several years. The importance of the Breath of God in the creation story of humans, the fifty trillion cells that make up just one adult body, the Christmas baby in the Bethlehem crèche and the hope that someday I will see my Creator, face to face, shout out from several different pages penned at very different times. These are theological and scientific facts that have been incorporated into these expressions of my faith. Poets take liberties by formulating new words (often constrained by the demands of rhyme) to express their thoughts. The meanings of these new expressions are usually self-evident but have been written in *Italics* to alert the reader.

# WHO AM I AND HOW IT ALL HAPPENED

I N THIS SECTION I have assembled thirteen of my musings that address the question of who I am and how did I happen. Most of my understanding of who I am is derived from my faith and primarily from the Judeo-Christian teachings. Most of my understanding about my physical composition and how I think is derived from both the Bible and God's revelation in the sciences. Geophysics tells us that all physical matter was created some 13-14 billion years ago at an important moment in time now called the Big Bang. In fact, most cosmologists believe that time (chronology) as we know it was also created in that instance. I can believe that the process of reducing such a vast amout of energy ($E = mc^2$) into the particles and elements that constitute our universe today took a very long time according to precise physical laws and that human life appeared at the very end of this time. In fact, the sequence of creation events taught by modern science is identical to the sequence of events told as metaphor in the book of Genesis. That nuclear physics, astrophysics, plate tectonics and glaciation played a role in the creation of our planet earth is strongly indicated by what is observed. That living systems came along as the ultimate creation is also not surprising but just how and why this happened requires more than what the scientific method can offer. The book of Genesis teaches that God breathed His Breath into humans in a way that was very different from anything else he created. That Breath has made us into *mini-Gods* with the capacity to do our own creating and to know right from wrong. What we take for granted in the physical gadgets that surround us was designed and created by humans over many years. Our homes, our cars, our clothing and other belongings were all designed by humans, then manufactured and promoted for sale to us. Most of us have bought into this system of modern business as if it was here from the start. But is wasn't. Cutting down trees for building shelters and heating homes was relatively easy. Our ability to purify single elements from the dirt of the earth, to refine the same and to form these products into gadgets with meaning has been a much harder haul. And most advances came after humans learned how to harness energy in the form of electrical power that could be delivered to all those regions that could afford it. So the idea that some creative power (God) designed what we see in our universe, including humans, requires no big "leap of faith". The order in our universe requires an ordering mind. The question of how these creations took place and for what purpose requires knowledge in addition to what we derive from the physical sciences. And philosophers and theologians have consistently addressed these matters for many years but have not come to a consensus at this time. Thus the strong hand of science and engineering has met many needs of current society which worships individualism and materialism and some scientists now concede that a God is no longer required. The arrogance of successful science and the timidity of faith-based approaches must share the blame for this current impasse.

Popular science today teaches that humans are the product of a Godless evolution whose molecular arrangements are some minimum of energy on their way to greater randomness, a process that takes about eighty years for persons born in the developed world. Why speeding up the process or early death is found objectionable by these folks is hard to understand. The Bible teaches that humans were created as the paramount of a Godly scheme whose duty is to worship the creator according to their moral precepts. That faith also teaches that our time in this space-time domain is brief but our being (soul) will live on beyond our physical deaths. The search for true meaning to one's life then demands attention to both the physical story of reality and the spiritual story of who we are and why we are. The words in the following poems attempt to focus our thoughts on these big issues and are the best that this poet's mind can produce. And this section of the book begins with something of the sanctity of words and why they should not be trivialized in any way. They are the backbone of the honest communication required to produce meaning and understanding.

# A Spoken Word

The power of a spoken word transcends
When voiced with an *unforked* tongue
Or even set to music, when it's sung
Conveys the precise meaning it intends
Communication is a special treasure
That's thoughtlessly invoked and oft' misused
The meaning of some words become abused
When cleverness is used to distort measure
Be circumspect about your choice of words
Attempt to maximize the message they convey
And only vocalize the ones that you discern
So that discourse can be loftier than that of birds
That truth be found in symbols you relay
And you never need to wish for their return

2002

# Discourse

That we can interact with others
So that our thoughts are known to them
Is a gift of incomparable worth
We sometimes take for granted
Those unique grunts and sounds
That can encode our very essence
We learn to transmit from mouth and lips
Unique sound waves that travel through space
To impact on some hearer's ear
Those sounds are then transduced
Resulting in the brainwaves used
To reconstruct true meanings for communications
Creating pictures on the flat screen of our brain
We're taught to compose words with symbols
That when printed on various materials
Are ingested by the eyes
Again these shapes are instantly transduced
To signals used to reconstruct the meaning
Of the true message intended by the writer
These discourse skills, best demonstrated by Jesus,
Require practice and maintenance
To guarantee that our communications will have integrity
But the ultimate purpose of these cryptic tools
Is to reveal the nature of that One
Who came as the True Word to inform about God

2005

# Nothingness

It takes a lot of faith for my atheist friends
To believe that human life has no worth
But our awareness span with its busyness
Cries for meaning to the fact of each birth
Are the fifty trillion cells of which I am composed
Just the product of mitotic division?
And the DNA code that determines my traits
Just a random gene template with no mission?
It's a fact that these bundles of metabolic might
Have a penchant to create and to love
To make secure bonds with other bundles
In communities with guidance from above
I'm so glad that I have been given the faith
To believe in a world that was planned
By a Super Creator who knows every detail
And deigned that this planet should be manned
By the likes of you and me who were merely dust
Until enlivened by His breath for a reason
I have a unique purpose in this glorious scheme
Eternal life at the end of my season

2014

# That Cycle of Dust

Most folks for years have peeked
To learn something of the mortal drama
Played out each day on personal stages, both distant and near
The daily influx of new beings
Into this lengthy play
Requires unending revisions to the initial plot and text

That molecular dust can be and is arranged
Into objects we call humans
Continues to confound the most brilliant and serious of thinkers
And we actors in this play
Find it hard to accept that our lives, our hurts and our joys,
Possess only a transient meaning

In fact, we wish we didn't have to see
The recycling of those enlivened dust-forms
Back to their primal state
But death has a reality as sure as birth
It stalks us on this stage of daily living
Effects a fearful exit in an early or in a later act

Who wrote this play? I was not asked to act!
Who placed me on this stage that ends in death?
I want no part of this molecular dance!
But could dust, the stuff of life, have greater meaning?
That the perceived is not the total scene?
Who will authenticate this role I now perform?

The good news, taught by our Savior
Is that I have an everlasting purpose to my unique spirit
That one created when His breath and my dust particles combined
The drama of eternal consequence is not just what is seen
But includes the invisible play of our *God-like* spirits
In which I star and strut my holy substance

2005

# Shackled by the Fourth Dimension

Time
That line upon which
We live our lives
Flows only in one direction
As we perform our earthly roles
We've been bound
Into a space
Where cause and effect
Where action and reaction
Lead us ever onward
Towards a dusty end
But God
Knows past, present and future
As the here and now
And death will free us
From this riddle of the temporal
Into His Holy Presence
Where the redeemed
Will bask in His eternal light
And days and nights
And passing years
Will be no more
When we see Him face to face

2007

# God's Big Bang

We might never know just why He acted
To set this cosmic scheme in motion
From focal and condensed energy
The sum of which staggers the mind
But ever since, those billion galaxies
Created in a flash of power
Have raced apart into the void
Of an infinite nothingness
Each galaxy contains a billion stars
That light and heat their unique planets
Which are tethered to these worldly centers
By precise gravitational force

It was on one planet that He produced
An abundance of living plants and creatures
That grew and reproduced by programs
Encoded in their DNA molecules
We're told that at one point in time
He breathed His breath into one creature
The *super-being* of all of His creation
The keeper of His flora and His fauna
His breath combined with physical molecules
Made little *god-like* creatures of us all
With powers for discernment of what's just
With knowledge of both right and wrong

When with the passing of some time
These little gods chose independence
God sent His son to planet earth
To reconcile these creatures to His love
He died a cruel death for their atonement
But from that grave arose to justify
And after His return back to his Father

He breathed again His Spirit to empower
Amazing love, how can it be?
That God almighty should first create
And then find us in our time and space
To bring us His salvation

2007

# Meditations at the Grand Canyon

The muddy river wends its turbid course
One mile below
Constrained within a chasm
Lined by painted walls
A moving panorama that is
Fodder for the skeptic and believer

The morning light shines only
On a portion of the story
While downward rays at noon
Probe to its deepest depths
And setting sun sets
Every part aglow

The colored strata tell of ages past
When earth was bathed in teeming seas
Their sediments revealed
By water rushing to a lower ground
Exposing all the secrets
Of our distant past

And others see the handiwork of God
Directly molding each and every wall
Placing the peaks and gorges
In their intended places
An awesome sign of His
Majestic power and sovereignty

Both skeptic and believer dare to dwell
God's presence permeates its heights and depths
And how this shrine was made
Is known only by the creator
Who draws man to Himself
By acts of power, love and grace

1998

# It's Just About Time

An app that lets us separate the past, from now and beyond
Like little cues to indicate events that come around
So we can organize our lives with somewhat true intention
God made it so when at creation He made the fourth dimension
He knew that we would benefit from a sequence to our living
To distinguish those events, our receiving and our giving
It's New Year's Day so learn to label upcoming things pristine
We've moved along our timing path to two thousand and fifteen
Not that this day will be different from the one that went before
It's just the next bar in the symphony of our life's musical score
And what eternal life will be is hard for us to define
But this is our hope that He has assured when we cross that line
We are so blessed to experience time as a part of his creation
But when He comes to recreate this world
we will know supreme elation

2015

# Is There Meaning to My Life?

Thousands of trillions of atoms, locked in molecular patterns
That form structures and functions
For only a while
These interact to cause my beginning, my growth
My life and my demise within
A span of about eighty years
I am a transient state of energetic particles that
Longs for greater randomness
And a higher entropic life
And as this thermodynamic quirk, I pass my time
Waiting for some stochastic vibration
To prod me onward
The mathematics that describes this state of transience
Assigns no meaning
To this molecular dance


A God whose power is greater than all comprehension
Created me from dust He'd made
For higher purpose
Then breathed His breath into this lifeless form
To fill me with awareness of the divine
With whom I can commune
My daily living has predestined purpose
A unique role within God's earthly kingdom
A reason for my life
So I pray for wisdom to discover in the teachings
Of His ambassador and Son, the Christ
How I should love
And the best news of this Holy paradigm
Is that my life will be eternal
In His recreated kingdom


2000

# Why Am I Aware?

This life within me has the power of awareness
A consciousness that knows of mine and theirs
Defined by cells composed of physical matter
Together which show joy and fear, but cares
Could fifty trillion cells just grow together?
To organize the tissues of each being
Form into groups that specialize in sensing
Our feeling, smelling, tasting, hearing, seeing
And if we simply are random assemblage
Of atoms with some prior life or not
What gives their current residence in my form?
A meaning that is worthy to be sought

The fact that I have power to imagine
To see my life as more than ion states
Gives me a sense there's value in my person
That defines, muses, dwells and contemplates
And why if I am only a molecular array
Some meta-stable minimum of energetics
Do I waste my time considering the others?
Attempt to interact with love and good phonetics
My quest to live at peace with fellow man
Surely implies a bond between our beings
To form a larger cohort of believers
That's called the Church, a body of *agreeings*

I'd much prefer a system of formation
By some designer with intelligence
Creating me for bidding His intentions
For causing me to revel in romance
Like Abraham, Moses, David and Christ Jesus
Who were knit together for a Holy cause
I have faith that my person is of value

Not just a recluse born of thermodynamic laws
I may never know exactly how I came to be
But my inner being tells me I should care
That a higher being with a loftier game plan
Has created me so that I will be aware

2013

# Who Am I?

Just as the Psalmist years ago
As he observed his immediate world
And marvelled at the fields and hills
Where the sun and stars had been hurled
It was obvious to him that this ordered state
Had been planned by some designer
With precision of beauty that staggered the mind
With components that couldn't be finer
While basking in this moment of meaning
This observer of earth and sky
Cried from the depth of his awareness
What can it all mean, who am I?

And psalmists today know extensive details
Of the cells that compose just one being
Some fifty trillion of these matter packets
Can account for our dreaming and seeing
That such an array of metabolic might
Works together to distinguish the whole
Astounds those that study the workings of men
Their purpose, their meaning, their role
Most complex systems in this modern world
Were designed by the intellect of men
I believe that my being was created by God
He knows the which, whys and when

2014

# The Wonder of It All

Supersonic electrons
Buzzing around in valence orbitals
Mating with those of other atoms
To produce molecules with unique meaning
These bits of matter form
The living cells that knit together
And function as the whole
That's known as ME
Structure and order
Are essential at the molecular,
The cellular and the tissue levels
If I am to be alive
And my being
Is superimposed upon this myriad
Of metabolic processes
Played out in an aqueous sea
Into this microscopic dust
God breathed His breath
That bound this physical mass
Into a unique person
I hurt, I cry, I love
Because my soul
Is made by the creator
And longs for new breath
From that life-giving Breather

2004

# Distractions With No Meaning

Away with things designed to distract
Our musings on eternal things
They titillate and pass the time
With trivia and short-lived wonders
We willingly satiate each waking hour
With busyness deemed to be essential
To mute the longing deep within
That wonders at the meaning on one's being
Can all creation have a focal plan?
A meaning for the mountains, valleys, rivers
The suns, the moons, the stars above
And complex systems we deduce to be alive
We've learned that atoms form the basis of all matter
They aggregate to form the building blocks
Of all the physical reality that we observe
Some that has life and other dust that doesn't
That some creator said, "Let there be light"
And quantum physics jumped to His command
That some creator said, "Let there be matter"
And atoms formed with different electronic states
That some creator said, "Let there be living creatures"
And biochemistry produced the goods
That some creator said, "Let there be Godlike beings"
Then breathed His love into my life for purpose
I can believe

2014

# THE INVASION OF GOD
# INTO HIS CREATION

S INCE GROWING UP in a small town on the Canadian prairies I still become extremely excited each time the Christmas season rolls around. Of course as a child I was enamored by all the festivities and particularly by the presents under our Christmas tree that were addressed to Donnie. I received both practical gifts of clothing and many of the new toys that I had observed in the catalogues of the department stores. That was before the days Walmart built their mega-stores in the smaller towns like mine. Catalogue shopping and the wait for delivery of the purchase by Canada Post was exciting and worked quite well. On-line shopping today is a reversion to that old process. In addition to those standard Christmas trappings, my parents made sure that we went to Church and learned about the coming of a Savior into this world. I took part in Christmas pageants and sang the carols with gusto since I had been blessed with a voice that could carry a tune. It was when I was a teenager and was planning for university that the facts of the incarnation took on a deeper meaning. This baby in a crèche whose coming we celebrate at Christmastime grew up to become a man that claimed to be the true Jewish Messiah (fulfilling the promises of the Old Covenant) and the Son of God. Wow! If this claim is true, one best sit up and listen to what He says. And what He said has been recorded by multiple witnesses and first century historians.

In this section of this book I have assembled seventeen poems that were written over several years to address the enormity of this historical event. That any god would lower himself to the level of his creatures just to tell them of their true meaning and hope is astounding. "For God so loved the world that He gave His only begotten Son" were words I memorized in Sunday school many years ago. And although His example was exemplary, most of His communication was through words. These have been recorded in as trustworthy a manner as any historical events of the first century. So each year (almost) I compose a poem that expresses some aspect of this monumental event that captures my thinking at that moment. There is no doubt in my mind that the incarnation (God becoming a human) is the pivotal point in history. In fact, we date all historical events as pre (BC) or post (AD) the time of His coming knowing now that the exact date may be off by a few years. And today there is a very active effort by non-believers to alter this dating system so as not to give significance to the importance of this event. The words of Jesus Christ are the words of God Almighty and should be heeded. Some of the greatest minds of their day came to this conclusion. C. S. Lewis, the great literary mind of the twentieth century and F. S. Collins, the great molecular biologist of today propound this truth in their various writings (in words). So while the vast majority of physical scientists are too busy to devote much time to spiritual matters, some of the best have discovered the incarnation to contain the true meaning of life on earth. Get excited about Christmas!

# A Risking God

God risked his plan for fallen man
When you and me he named
Ambassadors of his good news
So his love could be proclaimed
The message of redeeming grace
His death on Calvary
Absolves man of his vilest sin
His blood has paid for me
He placed his Spirit into these
Imperfect earthen vessels
A treasure rare, of utmost worth
With which our ego wrestles
Upon these broken forms he draped
His robes of righteousness
Adopted us, as his own sons
And heirs, what glorious dress
To be so loved by God above
Is hard to understand
The role for man in his grand plan
Seems surely out of hand
Yet God has made our task to tell
Of his salvation free
He risked creation's aims and goals
By loving you and me

2001

# The Miracles of Christmas

In the stillness of a stable
Witnessed by the oxen, sheep
A child was born to travelers
Who could find no place to sleep
Mary laid her boy-child Jesus
In a manger full of straw
And observed his mean condition
Filled with worship, wonder, awe
For his father was God's Spirit
And this babe, the Christ, God's Son
Would save his people from their sin
God came to His creation

To the tranquil of a hillside
On that cool crisp starry night
Where some shepherds watched their flocks
Huddled round their campfire bright
Came an angel of the Lord God
In a blinding haze of glory
To announce the news of Jesus' birth
And foretell salvation's story
These men made haste to Bethlehem
And found the babe with mother
Then glorified as they returned
And worshipped God their father

In the lab of learned wise men
Shone a brilliant star one night
Causing wonder and confusion
Since their charts showed none that bright
These three followed this enigma
The star led them to the place
Where Mary and the Christ-child were

Wise men fell down on their face
And worshipped Him the King of Jews
Their gifts to Him presented
Of gold and frankincense and myrrh
They had found the Lord's anointed

To the hearts of wearied people
In the various walks of life
At those times of desperation
Weighted down with grief and strife
Comes the Word of God with power
Telling of a Christ that came
Every ache and need he heals
Life need never be the same
When in faith we fall and worship
Like the shepherd and the sage
We can find our God incarnate
Like His saints throughout all age

It was miracle that God should come
To man in human body
And that angel choirs in concert
Should announce salvation story
It was miracle that learned men
By the brilliant star were led
That God should choose to indwell man
So His Kingdom can be spread
Pray all people at this season
Stop - and let His guiding light
Lead them to this Babe in worship
Find in Him, their joy and might.

1975

# He Has Made Himself Known

What does it mean that I get up each morning?
And jog about doing my things?
Am I just a collection of molecular bits?
That studies, and argues and sings
When I look at the breadth of the cosmic array
Is my being just a spec in that mixture?
Or is there more to what's seen, the real in between,
This physical and spiritual fixture?

Thank God that He came to tell of His plan
Was incarnate as a babe in a crèche
Then grew up to teach, of a love that could reach
Through a message that was cogent and fresh
I was born for a purpose within His great scheme
His workman with seeds to be sown
I thank God that at Christmas we celebrate
His coming, when He made Himself known

2010

# If You Can Believe

If you can believe that some almighty power
Designed all that we touch and we see
Each cell in our body was made from His matter
Each mountain, each river and galaxy
Has been placed in a space with a unique purpose
Whose vastness may never be known
That His breath was breathed into human forms
Making moral beings out of stone
If you can believe that this almighty power
Made we persons as the object of His affection
That He sent His own Son as a baby in a crèche
To grow up and teach of this connection
And since selfishness blinded the eyes of His loved ones
This Man, on a cross, died for sins
That sacrifice atones, can make us truly righteous
When in faith we repent, life begins
If you can believe that at Christmastime
We celebrate this great Advent of our Savior
The snowmen and Santa recede with the tinsel
Its import should condition our behavior
This Christmas let us pray for a simple faith
That will see a great God in a manger
Whose coming has provided the way to Yahweh
We no longer roam earth as a stranger

2014

# To Be So Loved

The message of this blessed time
Confounds our mortal minds discretely
We struggle with the consequence
Of being loved so total and completely
The friendships and relations
We form along the paths of life's endeavor
Are guarded and protected
To minimize the hurts, if they should sever
The love expressed in families
Between some husbands, wives and progeny
Is nearest that of the creator's
For his created, such divine charity
But in the main our time is passed
By selfish pursuit, me my major love
Oblivious to lasting goals
To things eternal and light from up above
Why we should be so loved by God
So boundless, free and unconditional
Is foreign to our fallen minds
Our justice, stern and *retributional*
And yet a trace of His sweet breath
Imparted to these forms at His creation
Still reaches out to the I AM
To be so loved by His unearned redemption

2004

# The Fullness of Time

In the fullness of time, that was
Known only to the Almighty
The humdrum of daily living
Was visited by the unexpected
A child was born
To parents who were on the road
To comply with an edict
From their governor
Bethlehem was crowded
Their room at the inn was a stable
Mary's labor pains couldn't wait
And God became incarnate
Why God should choose such lowly means
To usher in The Savior
Runs counter to the human way
It irritates man's logic
The Divine Light that first shone that night
On cattle, sheep and oxen
Still dispels the darkness from our worlds
When we fall in adoration
The Word has come, God's voice was heard
And we can know redemption
God moved in this mysterious way
And shows His love to all

1999

# The Hope of the World Has Come

Oh come, oh come, Messiah
And liberate your people
Restore us to our Holy Land
And rule with majesty
Teach us to bow before you
To love our foes and brothers
So all the world will come to know
The One that sets man free
I came, I came, my children
Was born in lowly manger
And as a suffering servant
I taught and healed the land
Was crucified and buried
For all of your transgressions
Was resurrected to new life
Now sit at God's right hand
You come, you come, all seekers
Find Him to be your Savior
That babe of Bethlehem
Now crowned the King of Kings
Fall down with awe and worship
And don't resist His Spirit
That floods believers with new life
And causes us to sing

2002

# That God is Light

John's gospel tells that God is Light
What's meant by this bold teaching?
It helps to be a physicist
To understand this preaching
Light is a form of energy
Devoid of any matter
It travels at the fastest speed
Can be absorbed or scatter
And at the speed of light we're told
There is no need for time
The past, the present and what's to come
Become the now and prime
The temporal limits that frustrate man
Don't impact our Creator
He sees all history as now
He is the omniscient Spectator
And when His Light is scattered
Through the darkness of this earth
Illumination by God's truth
Can inform us of our worth
And when that Light becomes absorbed
Within each human being
It transforms us to the children of God
We can have supernatural seeing
So at this Christmastime, rejoice
For the coming of God's Light
That shone on the darkness of my sin
And made me holy in God's sight

2004

# It Staggers the Mind

To think that God
All power that our human minds would dare to comprehend
Would deign to come to earth
Accept the limits of a human body
And suffer death
To tell us of His plan of love
Why should any god
Violate the order of the here and out there
Intrude upon our trappings
Heal the blights man cannot cure
Feed the hungry with a lasting nurture
And invert the social order?
These outrageous actions
Run counter to the best of all man's reasoning
They upset our human niceties
The correctness we all strive for
They make explicit our finiteness
In the light of Holy wisdom
Could it be that the Creator
Holds the blueprint for a global plan?
Where His creatures are so loved
. And are wooed to the extreme
Until they can't resist to bask
In the arms of their Maker

2004

# How Can It Be?

How can it be that the God of this earth
Should come to His world as a baby?
Constrained by the limits of tissue and bone
The confusion, the questions and the maybe
Why would someone with infinite power
Choose to weaken His might and domain?
To subject himself to the tools of man
To succumb to their hope, love and pain
Why would the creator of physical matter
Get wrapped up in His own creation?
Diminish his role as the power out there
To humble himself to man's station

The miracle of Christmas is more than it seems
We worship divine incarnation
God's purpose was clear, He needed a path
For a vital communication
That told of His love for the creatures He'd made
Their importance in His cosmic plan
With Him they will rule on an earth that's redeemed
His purpose for each woman and man
So this Christmas we worship, we sing, we adore
We marvel with wonder at His birth
For in Bethlehem's stall, God declared to all
His love for his creatures and their worth

2008

# A Mighty and Blessed Coalescence

Bleating goats and sheep and mooing cows
With soggy bales of hay in the damp and dingy darkness
A young couple seeking refuge from the dank and chill of night
Their breaths in expectant puffs viewed in cool evening air
Not seen by human eye not heard by human ear
God's Spirit moving on this set to bring mankind salvation
A baby's cry, a mother's warm caress
Their son, our Savior, had arrived in a lowly cattle stable
Shepherds came to worship and angel choirs sang loudly
The kings from the east paid tribute to this King
This awesome coalescence of the earthly and the heavenly
Declares throughout the ages that the Son of God has come
So graft yourself into this scene, drink deep redemption's message
Ingest the Word of God made flesh, find new life at His manger

2011

# Christmas Ifs

If the angels of the heavens took the time to sing
At the birth of a babe in a manger
And the angelic hosts hovered over Bethlehem
As the place for the coming of a Savior
Why is it hard for us common folks
To believe in a God that came
To show us His grace and love as never before
In a world that would never be the same

If the wise men of the east were confused by the signs
And journeyed to that crèche to discover
The King of the Jews in such humble estate
An enigma for their minds to uncover
Why is it difficult for the learned of today
To accept this divine incarnation
To fall on our faces and worship the one
Who played out the plan of salvation

If the shepherds on that hillside were drawn to the site
Of the birth of the Holy of Holies
And journeyed to that barn to give just honor
To the One who had been sent from the glories
Why is it wrong for persons in this world
To approach Him with honor and praise
To laud the arrival of Creator to His creatures
To discover the real meaning for our days

We can argue the details of each of these events
And analyze the minutia of the past
But what is required is to fall down in fear
And pray for a faith that will last
Why God became man is beyond our comprehension

That He should love his created is far out
But for those who believe in this Christmas miracle
It behooves us to sing, dance and shout

2013

# Take Off Your Shoes

How can it be that Almighty God
Would choose to confine His glory?
To the body of a baby of lowly birth
To bring us salvation's story
How can it be that the Savior of men
Should burst on our scene unexpected?
To nurture and love the rich and the poor
And the many this world had rejected
What can explain such passionate love
The Creator comes to woo His creatures?
Our worth is declared by this ominous birth
It confounds the best of our teachers
Why would a holy, omnipotent God
Show up as a babe in a crèche?
When all of His angels and heavenly hosts
With light, could have dazzled all flesh
Our answers are thread-bare, it's hard to just wrap
Our minds 'round this grand provocation
God's ways are not ours, it behooves us to heed
This miracle of His incarnation
At all of those glorious moments in time
When God's glory was uniquely displayed
A Holy fear gripped the humble observers
They knelt, they prostrated, they prayed
Just like Moses, when he stood at that burning bush
Where no natural explanation was found
"Take your shoes off", and worship this child
You are standing on Holy ground

2005

# Worship the Babe of Bethlehem

At an unsuspecting time
In a most unusual place
Almighty God arrived
As a baby in a stable
Constrained by human form
Within both time and space
He lived a life of love
Our salvation to enable
Why God would choose to condescend
To the level of His creatures
Confounds superior reason
And offends the rigorous mind
We'd prefer a lofty power
Not an interfering presence
A god who stays out there
But is loving, just and kind
The intrusion of the Divine
Into the ways of men
Was accomplished to communicate
And demonstrate His grace
We should fall before the manger
Full of reverence, fear and awe
Let His Spirit fill our lives
As we humbly view God's face


2001

# Christmas Morning

Awake believers, greet the day
When the promised Messiah came
Not riding on a royal steed
Enrobed as a king to reign
But as a babe of lowly birth
Was bedded in cattle manger
Among his parents, oxen, sheep
He came just like a stranger
Awake believers, greet the Light
That on this day did shine
Illuminates our darkest hours
With brightness of the Divine
When we in faith direct our hearts
To this radiance of the heaven
We too will know of saving grace
And why a Son was given
Awake believers, greet the Word
Revealed as flesh to flesh
God's message to a fallen race
Lay swaddled in a crèche
This Word transforms all those that hear
His blood can be redeeming
When we at Christmastime bow down
To the Savior who brings true meaning

2002

# Kairos, God's Time (Galatians 4:4)

In a very special place, in the fullness of God's time
Emmanuel arrived in His creation
He came to witness to God's love and teach us purpose
To be sacrificed, atone for our salvation
Just when and how God makes His moves
Is beyond our deepest comprehension
But make no mistake, He is on His throne
And our life events are timed by His intention
We try to manage all the details of our lives
To maximize our comforts, control our goals
Fill our days with work and pleasures that distract
As if on stage we act out many roles
But the times and ways of God unknown to us
His omniscience and sovereignty stand apart
Someday we'll know the value of His moves
And where to place the horse and place the cart
God's sovereign powers on earth most vividly displayed
When our life on earth comes to its final end
He calls us home, that blessed hope fulfilled
To a kingdom life with Christ our Savior, friend

2015

# The Residue of Christmas

When all of the tinsel and lights come down
And the glitter is stripped away
When the left-over turkey has seen its last meal
And life becomes normalcy
Was anything learned from this bold extravaganza?
This materialistic invention
Where commercial is blended with spiritual
To capture our vivid attention
It was good to have visited family and friends
A bonding of our innermost selves
Some gifts that were given might meet our just needs
While others will be placed on our shelves
Did the spin of the season cause undo stress?
From the dashing to events to and fro
Just to keep family ritual by hook or by crook
Sometimes in the sleet and the snow
But Advent is the season to remember Christ's coming
Did He come this year to your home?
And Christmas reminds us of a God that so loved
Became incarnate, left His glorious throne
Through all of the ribbons, flashing lights and the feast
The pageants of shepherds and the crèche
I pray you were visited in some special way
By our Savior, the Word become flesh

2005

# STORIES JESUS TOLD AND GODLY COMMUNICATIONS

THE TWENTY-TWO POEMS in this section contain my musings on what Jesus taught His followers and our response to those teachings. Some are paraphrases of His parables and several deal with themes from both the Old and New Testaments.

Jesus taught by telling stories and using metaphors. Most of the Old Testament is one big story of how God chose to reveal His moral character through the example of one people, Israel, and there are many choice parts that I was shielded from in my Sunday school story telling. It was through that Jewish nation that the promised Messiah, Jesus the Christ, would come to tell of a New Covenant and redeem all ethnicities into His church of believers. And each teaching form utilized words in sentences that would have been understood by the hearers. So words, probably in Aramaic in the case of Jesus, are the sacred vehicle by which we learn of the physical world and also the spiritual role of humans within it. Thus, the telling and retelling of the most important stories of creation in words that everyone can understand should resonate with enquiring minds. And there are certainly many aspects of this wonderful story that have not been given prominence in these poems. My understanding of my life expands each day and I will be searching for meaning until I die. It is hoped that some of my musings can be useful in your meditations as you contemplate who you are and why you are here. The process of writing down in meaningful words what one thinks and believes is a good exercise for everyone. Each person has the capacity to become a poet.

# By What Authority?

The gospel's claims are brash and bold
That God came down to earth we're told
And suffered death deserved by me
His substitution sets one free
Can one believe such huge contention?
This awesome act provides redemption?
For sure, 'tis truth declared befit
FOR THE MOUTH OF THE LORD HAS SPOKEN IT

The goodness in man's heart is slight
He tries to love with all his might
But love one's foe and enemy
As perfect as my love for me?
Who can fulfil this bold demand?
This edict that seems out of hand
Fall down before His throne with laud
THIS IS THE STANDARD OF OUR GOD

And judgement in the end will come
Our fate, determined by the sum
Not of the deeds of good we've acted
But through the grace that Christ transacted
Can such insurance be believed?
Does God vouchsafe by grace received?
His Son's own blood was shed to give
AND JESUS BIDS, "BELIEVE AND LIVE"

And still today God's word is spoken
His Spirit woos each heart that's broken
The message is the same, unchanged
That man from God became estranged
But through divine initiative

He made a way that we might live
What proof is there for all to see?
A GOD WHO SPEAKS, WITH AUTHORITY

2000

# In Search For What Is Holy

"There's nothing sacred in this world"
Rings loud and clear today
The search for hallowed saints or grounds
Is an exercise in disarray
Where should one delve to contemplate
The sinless, what is holy?
Or does our innate fallen state
Preclude such acts as folly?

The Hebrews in a bygone age
Knew of Shekinah glory
*Presenced* in, around and above the ark
That secured laws and the covenant story
This awesome place provoked Holy fear
Which over time, could make people wise
And the presence of Yahweh, Almighty God,
Demanded reverence, laud, honor and disguise

But when Jesus was crucified upon the cross
The veil in the temple was rent
Exposing all mortals to the Light of this World
Creating clean hearts, God's intent
And in those who have opened their life to this Word
The holiness of God now abounds
Making righteous and pure the sinner most vile
Such undeserved grace now astounds

I fall on my knees Lord, give thanks everyday
For renewing my heart, pure and free
I pray that you'll wash my life whiter than snow
Through Your Spirit that now dwells in me

And I'm chastened to know that your love in this world
Now radiates from Your Body, the Church
And the holiness that I set out to find
Is in me, there's no need for my search

2000

# Unearned and Undeserved Grace

(A father and a son, Luke 15: 11-32)

He watched him leave
That second son who chose to go his way
With his inheritance in hand
To learn how others play
The father's heart was heavy
With the pathos of the moment
He wondered what he might have done
To avoid this anguish torrent
The son rushed to excitement
He never looked behind
Was intent to taste of pleasures
From the world he was to find
At first his life was joyful
And his senses were aroused
He bought his friendship with others
As he partied, danced, caroused
His excessive celebration
Made him the focus of attention
And he never really stopped to think
'Bout the meaning or intention
He spent the lot on fun and games
Had a taste of sexual pleasure
It didn't take that long for him
To squander the family treasure
Without the monies that had bought
Him transient companions
He had to earn a living
Feeding pigs with husks and onions
It was in this sty that he looked back
To those in his father's employ
They had shelter, food and security

A life they could almost enjoy
He wondered if his father
Would be willing to take him back
As a worker in his fields
So he filled up his pack-sack
The long trek home was filled with doubts
He had lived a life of deception
And wondered what his dad would say
At that tense upcoming reception
But the father had looked down that path each day
On which his son had departed
And prayed to God that he would return
So relationship could be restarted
And when in the distance he caught a glimpse
Of a figure that looked like his son
He went out to meet him, with heart full of joy
And eventually broke into a run
He embraced this prodigal son with love
The boy started his prepared confession
But it wasn't required to heal the hurts
The son learned a mighty big lesson
That the love of a father for his begotten
Is a bond that is hard to sever
Forgiveness was complete and evident
For the one who had been so clever
A party was ordered to celebrate
The return of the one gone astray
The best robe and ring were placed on the lad
He knew that he wanted to stay
This parable teaches that the love of God
For each member of his creation
His daughters and sons who leave the fold
To seek worldly pleasure and station
Is so great that he sent His only son
To die on a cross in our place

And when we return to our rightful home
We are showered with His love and His grace
We can start afresh in relationship
Like a father accepts a new child
Knowing we are treasured, the apple of His eye
Redeemed, forgiven, reconciled

2007

# Water, the Solvent of God

(John 4: 1–30)

That life in God's creation is conducted in solution
Whether it be plant or animal in form
Speaks loudly of foreknowledge of the laws of biochemistry
Where reactions in a solvent are the norm
Man spends his billion dollars to inquire of the planets
Whether water is now present or was there
Since he can't conceive of life in anything not aqueous
As if a sovereign God would really care

So mankind as he's created consists of mainly water
But his other molecules play major roles
In their growing and begetting in their loving and regretting
When they contemplate and learn eternal goals
Is $H_2O$ a component of the likeness of our Maker?
That was imposed upon our dust when once he breathed
His life into our forms at the moment of creation
When our roles within His purpose was conceived?

Each day our bodies drink in several liters of this good stuff
To maintain our different cells in form that's fit
To deny replenishing this essential solvent of our being
Would reduce us surely to a piece of grit
And although mankind has learned of several details of the process
Whereby invisible reactions within our cells
Maintain our being and our health by laws He sanctioned
We go on drilling deeper wells

We know the power water has in the role of body cleansing
And mothers know it works on Monday washday
Dilution has always been a solution to pollution
With water the solvent choice if done the right way

That seventy percent of the surface of our planet
Consists of water found in rivers, seas and lakes
Attests to its importance in God's plans for His creation
We should guard against its fowling by mistakes

But the woman at the well was taught by Jesus
Of an everlasting water that He can give
One that won't evaporate in the heat of our trials
And all we have to do is drink and live
And the life this water generates is eternal
It's His Holy Spirit that He pours out to indwell
And our mission in His plan for all creation
To draw neighbors to this deep, deep Holy Well

2012

# Come and See the One

## (John 4: 7-30)

In the heat of the noon she had come to the well
To draw water required for that day
When a stranger, a Jewish man, asked for a drink
Placing all their social rules in disarray
He spoke of living water, something greater than the content
Of this Jacob well revered for many years
Then recited all her past that was not so glorious
She was startled and experienced great fears
Who was this interloper and what did he mean?
What kind of living water was His to give?
Could this woman's sins be pardoned,
could her life be turned around?
Would one drink beget new life for her to live?
She remembered then her teachings of a promised Messiah
One who would liberate her people from *repression*
If this was He, as He claimed to be
The folks in town should know of His position
She rushed into her town and shouted, "Come and see
The One" who knew the details of her sordid past
She witnessed to the fact that Messiah might have come
To bring a righteous kingdom that would last
Many persons believed Him to be the Promised One
Invited Him to stay, to teach the way
All because one unsuspecting women at Jacob's well
Met the source of Living Water at noon day

2016

# A Very Special Lamb

(Luke 15: 3-7)

The rosy glow of setting sun
Illuminated well the evening sky
As temperatures cooled the valley floor
That nightly haven for his meandering sheep
When all the lambs were in the fold
The shepherd did a final count
Only to find there were ninety and nine
One short of the number of his small flock
After placing his crook across the gate
To make sure that none would escape
He ventured out deep into rugged hills
Where his animals had been feeding
He searched 'til the sun had stopped giving light
He listened for any tale-telling bleats
It was well into night when he almost gave up
And returned to his remaining sheep
Then a soft hurtful baa directed him to
His lamb that was lodged in crevasse
He rescued the beast, he cuddled him close
And carried it home on his shoulder
These words of our Shepherd tell well of our worth
He ventured into our messy world
To tell of His plan to rescue each person
So that His enfolded flock will be complete

2016

# It Is Finished

"IT IS FINISHED", those words of fear and dread
The last before our Savior bowed His head
Upon a cross. What shameful death He died
The sequel to those haunting words he cried.

Could man obstruct the mission of his God?
The one who demands worship, praise and laud
A God who sent His Son to Calvary
To die our death? So grace can set us free.

Those words imply finality, an end
But those who claim His grace will comprehend
Atonement for their guilt and all their sinning
Redeemed by love, it's surely a beginning.

1998

# How Can Death Be Good?

We learn more detail of Christ's final hours
Than the rest of His thirty some years
The lashes, the nails, the garden, the pathos
The cries to His Father for survival
But then He was tortured and hung
On that despised cross of execution
His death was unjustified and illegal
Innocent life was taken by the Roman soldiers and the crowd
And then we dare to call it GOOD FRIDAY
The breath of this man in his prime was snuffed out
His disciples and followers faded back into the scene
His body was interred behind a massive stone
No wonder some philosophers and deep thinkers
Find no logic in these barbaric actions
And if He truly was this earth's Creator
His created beings killed the very Son of God
It's only when we learn of resurrection and ascension
That our Paschal Lamb is surely Triune God
And when His Spirit comes to dwell within us
Our lives can teach of all the good He taught
His death somehow atones for our transgressions
So that we become His righteousness and partner
And that crucifixion on that hill called Golgotha
Is our redemption and is VERY GOOD, indeed!

2016

# The Offence of the Cross

Yes, a crime was committed, innocent life was snuffed out
By the Romans and Jews in colleague
On a cross that was meant for the vilest of vile
What good could this injustice achieve?
To martyr one life for the peace of their people
Was the judgement of the scribes and Pharisees
And insurrection on the fringe of the Roman Empire
Was not easily managed by decrees
The fact that this charismatic was the Jewish Messiah
Was recognized by only a few
That His death would accomplish atonement for sin
Was a radical scheme, that was new
But the Calvary cross is symbolically offensive
Reeks of weakness, of shame and of guilt
How could such a man restore Israel's pride?
With dignity could David's city be rebuilt?
And to suggest that mankind required a Savior
That our individual rights be subjected
To a creator's plan, designed in the Heavens
Was not logic for the many that rejected
But God sent His Son to die in our stead
An ignoble and cruel sacrifice
If we can only believe in this atoning cross
Our salvation will be bought at great price

2015

# The Empty Tomb

(John 20: 1-18)

An empty tomb
The linens lay folded
On the slab where His body was laid
The women cried
"Who has taken our Lord?
What more of a price must be paid?"
It was Mary
As she lingered awhile
As she grieved for the loss of her Master
Asked the gardener
"Did you see the ones
Who have caused this shameful disaster?
But the gardener
Was Jesus who called out, "Mary"
And she knew it was her risen Lord
She rushed to the others
To share the good news
"He's alive, he's been true to His word"
To this day
He still calls everyone by their name
Stop and listen as he speaks to you
Jesus lives
He has conquered the power of death
He offers eternal life that is true

2004

# Fearfully and Wonderfully Made

My Lord, you've created this person in me
Unique, in God's image, made so fearfully
Enriched by Your Spirit through the life breath you gave
And so wondrously blessed when you chose me to save

My life has new meaning, to keep vital and whole
For the work of the Master, an integral role
In a mission with meaning, God's message to tell
To the injured and weak, to the sick and the well

I was called and am grafted to the family of God
That group of believers, redeemed through His blood
A role in this Body of Christ was assured
When I yielded my heart to the love in His Word

Some pastors, some teachers and those that give care
Make music, give offerings and kneel down in prayer
Unique in each service as His Word is proclaimed
All part of that body where Jesus is named

Fill my life with your Spirit and teach me to show
His love and forgiveness to friend and to foe
This vessel of earth at your feet I have laid
For I have been fearfully, wonderfully made

1997

# A God That Makes Clothing

Is He a tailor or a seamstress?
Sewing clothes from animal skins
Or should we take those words to mean?
God's method to cover human sins
Such menial work for an almighty God
With a needle and thread in His hand
Distracts from His awesomeness, His omniscience and power
It's so hard for we created to understand

The Genesis account is clear to say
God spoke, God breathed, God created
We God-like creatures in His image
For which His love has never abated
Our banishment from Eden was all he could do
To preserve the pure realm for His pleasure
He immediately set out on a plan to woo
The banished back into His treasure

It was through a chosen people that this plan was promulgated
Was instructed through their prophets, priests and kings
And then He sent His only Son, as the Word made flesh
To teach us 'bout the meaning of beginnings
He showed His love by healing, feeding, and forgiving
By washing feet just like a slave that served
And through His death He sewed us robes of righteousness
A glory that was surely undeserved

2015

# Held Safely in His Hands

The bumps and grind of modern daily living
Our lives in constant flux, subjects of change
Surrounded by the restless and the strange
We long for havens safe; we need forgiving
Where can one find a truth that's never altered?
A creed composed of all that's just and pure
A faith to meet each need, and yet secure
Within ourselves, amidst events so faltered?
The God of heaven and the earth can be your shield
His holy power becomes our strong deflection
His boundless grace floods into all the lands
It moves our hearts to worship and to yield
Our total self to His divine protection
Secured, within the hollow of His hands.

2005

# Quest for the Divine

When with our human consciousness
We dwell on the Divine
Our faculties seem overtaxed
Best efforts end up flawed
Can one know the mind of God?

By process of deduction
We reach out to find our Maker
Our realities are patterned
By descriptions of the physical
Can one realize the spiritual?

We cram our brains with data sets
Strive to know redundant facts
Then integrate our God-image
From figments of this collection
Is God just some introspection?

But Yahweh spoke his will to man
Through prophet, priest and king
He sent His only Son to tell
To succor from dependence
Do we question God's transcendence?

His Spirit floods into our hearts
Infiltrates our awareness
We're bathed in His redeeming blood
A gift that can't be earned
Does this jive with what we've learned?

Discovering that God's presence
Is at hand, inspires awe

He has made our quest for the Divine
An act of simple affirmation
Dare one reject such invitation?

1999

# The Voices of God

The voice of Love confronts us
As we move throughout our days
Almighty God addresses man
He speaks in different ways
His message of redeeming grace
Rings clear for all to hear
It comes to us in many ways
Not only through the ear
Our eyes perceive His glorious works
The grandeur of all nature
Some glimpse, a writing on the wall
While most have read some scripture
To touch a newborn baby's skin
Speaks wonders of creation
An arm to guide the needy blind
Tells of our Lord's compassion
The smell of grandma's biscuits
Baked especially for our stay
Proclaims His love through family bonds
In a most enjoyable way
We feast upon His providence
Oh, the taste of the divine
God comes to us in broken bread
And drinking of the wine
Receptors in our human forms
He made to sense His presence
And fellowship with God above
Is basic to man's essence

2001

# The Trees Sing His Praises

(Psalms 96:12)

Majestically clothed in fabrics of green
Which produce the breath for our being
The trees of the forest, creations of God
Have starred in his drama of redeeming
When man disobeyed an early law of God
And ate of the forbidden fruit
It was leaves from a tree that covered the shame
And were woven to produce his first suit
When cut into planks they constructed the ark
That Noah was commanded to prepare
It spared some believers from the waters of death
Salvation by floatation for each pair
When Moses was leading the children of God
Out of Egypt, like a shepherd tends his flock
God's power was revealed in a simple wood staff
To part sea and yield water from the rock
Dried branches positioned beneath goat and lamb
Were ignited in sacrificial blaze
Atonement for sin with life-giving blood
Was required by God, to appease
His laws were unalterably etched into stone
A standard we all fail to attain
They were guarded by wood of the covenant box
In the Holy of Holy domain
When God sent His Son to bring the good news
To accomplish his promise of grace
It was wood of a manger that cradled our Lord
First witnessed the love in His face
And in the fullness of time, on Calvary's mount
Where the Holy was sacrificed for all sins
The cross, formed from trees, was the tool of His death

It is there where new life begins
So stop in the forest and reverently pause
Observe these tall instruments of God
In the stillness of ferns and moss, listen as they
Sing their worship, their praise and their laud

2001

# Reworked Clay

(Jeremiah 18: 1-4)

When first by His strong hands was moulded
My life into a vessel filled with purpose
I did not see a pot of virtue nor of beauty
I marred it with my selfishness and ego

This world's creator, that sovereign potter
Has formed each person for His purpose
And as we try to shape our own intentions
We often end up shattering His intended work

But God pursues His creatures with a vengeance
He gathers all the potsherds of our broken being
Softens the clay of our intrinsic substance
Reshapes us into something He deems best

Lord, fill these vessels with your love and Spirit
May they find use within your Kingdom plan
Surround us with your mighty arms of power
And may we feel the potter's gentle hands

2010

# Whiter Than Snow

The air was cold and filled with flakes
It fell with little regard for gravity
Cladding each earthly object with a whiteness
That covered up the normal drab
This blanket of pureness obliterated
The earthly surface with all its human messes
And for those that live in lands of snow
We know that it is but a transient redemption
Beneath this cleansing cover lies the same
Our cluttered lives and sins of human busyness
You can be sure will reappear at time of melt
Revealing the true nature of our weakness
Oh that there was a washing much more lasting
To rid our lives of things at deepest depth
Not just a façade of a winter moment
A rooting out of all our sin and discord
The John of Patmos teaches of such cleansing
A clothing with the righteousness of God
How robes can be made white when dipped in red blood
Is a miracle availed by His Son's death
So when you see the whiteness of the snow this winter
Be reminded of those heavenly robes of purity
That were purchased by our Savior at Mt. Calvary
To blanket all mortal forms that will accept

2013

# Andrea at Her Christening

A helpless babe presented to the One
Who taught the crowd to "let the children come"
And warned of adult hindrance in the way
Of those who'd claim His Kingdom on this day

Obediently, with faith, the parents stand
As water washes from the pastor's hand
Onto her head. The awesome deed is done
Invoking all the might of Father, Spirit, Son

Beneath this rite so simple and reserved
Which often begs a reverence more deserved
The God of Life meets humans in their sin
Washes with Christ's blood, His Spirit rushes in

And all His Church rejoices for this day
The increase of Christ's Kingdom had its way
And pledges to be diligent and faithful
In nurturing this new life in the Gospel

1977

# The Bread and Wine

His body broken for man's sin
His lifeblood shed for me
In agony and pain he died
In my place on that tree
This substitution for my crime
My savior bore alone
Now I am free, this paschal lamb
For man's sins did atone

We gather at this altar now
Before the bread and wine
In penitence we kneel prepared
Partake of meal divine
The bread is broken like his flesh
Like blood, the wine is poured
Both are consumed to celebrate
The death of our dear Lord

This sacrament, first served by Christ
Is surely a remembrance
But more than that, to those who eat
It can become transcendence
God's spirit fills the bread and wine
Redeeming forces flow
Man's sins are washed away anew
And mortal Christians grow

1994

# So How Do We Handle Miracles?

Gallons and gallons of available water
Turned into a wine that was vintage
Persons with leprosy, palsy and blindness
Healed of their ailments by a touch
A man blind from birth can immediately see
Through eyes that were clouded and dead
And to top it all off, good old Lazarus
Awakens after four days of *rigor mortis*
Some want to believe that these are just tales
Told by the followers of Jesus
But historic consensus by multiple witnesses
Suggests that these events are all factual
How is one able to feed five thousand mouths
With only five buns and two fish
Have enough left over for the foodbank
In the hungry nearby city
What sort of person can still a strong wind
By a simple authoritative voice
Or know where the nets should be lowered
To obtain a record catch
An omnipotent, omniscient, all present God
Who designed the workings of His creation
Can no doubt modify every detail
By process beyond man's understanding

2016

# Caught Up In the Spirit

(The book of Revelation)

John saw into the heavens
When he was caught up in the Spirit
Was shown the wonders of God's plan, man's destiny
He saw a heavenly throne, surrounded
By two dozen praising elders
And four creatures covered with many eyes to see
Upon the throne was seated
One whose brilliance surpassed pure light
From his mouth there came a double-edged sword
Also centered in this throne
There was a Lamb that had been slain
Who was worthy to take and open up scrolled word
Both the elders and the creatures
Never ceased to sing their praises
To the one who was, and is, and is to come
And to the Lamb who had been slain
Whose blood had purchased men for God
And is now creating us a perfect home
As the seven seals were opened
John witnessed all the horrors
As four agents of the evil one laid waste
Pain and death that knew no limit
Was inflicted by these riders
King and peasant, rich and poor all had their taste
But the souls of all the martyrs
Cried out loud to God, how long?
Until our spilt blood can be avenged
They were given pure white robes
And told to wait a little longer
There were many more believers to be revenged
Then John saw a multitude of people

More than anyone could number
With palm branches in their hands and garbed in white
Singing praise to God and Lamb
Who had brought them out of tribulation
Whose blood had washed their robes and made them bright
But the best part of the vision
Was the coming of a Kingdom
That exemplified all that our minds find good
No more suffering, death or sorrow
In surroundings that are perfect
We will live forever in His perfect neighborhood
And our worship will flow freely
To the one whose blood atoned
For all the wrongs and hurts each life had done
We will share the purpose of our being
In His life and new creation
Eternal with the Father and the Son

2004

# BLENDING SCIENTIFIC DISCOVERY WITH FAITH

T HE TWENTY-THREE POEMS in this section were composed at various times over the past thirty or more years to express as clearly as possible my thinking on many matters. Some were prompted by visualizing my material surroundings, some were prompted with my handling moments of immediate emotions involving other persons and some were just outbursts. Near the end of this section, I have included a previously published poem, A POET'S CREED, written about forty years ago. It is a summary of Christian teaching that is orthodox and evangelical. I can honestly attest to the fact that after all my years of searching and intellectual endeavors, I can buy into all its words. Some poems that were written on the spur of the moment after hearing a sermon in church, after discussing some issue with a colleague or when viewing the wonders of the natural world. When one lives on the edge of Okanagan Lake in the mountains of Western Canada one is challenged each day with vistas *extraordinaire*. SWALLOWS IN SPRINGTIME flowed off my pen (which is really my computer) after observing the erratic movements of twenty or thirty such birds while drinking my morning coffee on our house deck that overlooks the lake. I don't know what they were up to but whatever it was they had accomplished by early afternoon when no birds were evidenced. To think that a large portion of the DNA of birds, the genetic code that directs the sequencing of their amino acids into proteins of function, is very similar to the DNA in cells of my body is sobering. Why can't I fly about to express such exhilaration? I was derived (created) from a line of mammals whose functions in this world are much different than that of birds. And humans have been infused with the "breath of God" which makes us unique in this world. I trust that some of these musings will provide a spark of excitement in your life and encourage you to write down your observations and feelings.

# What is God Like?

The idea of a God that should not be depicted
Confounds one's most basic intentions
How should we then apply our reasoning?
To imagine a power with no dimensions
We learn we're created in the image of God
Do I simply look into a mirror?
If that's all there is, then heaven help me
And even those that are moral and austere
So language is invoked to direct our thoughts
To His omnipotence, omniscience and omnipresence
The concepts of a judge and powerful king
Are used to demand our allegiance
But the fact that our musings define an "out there"
Makes our imagery hard to discern
Since all of our dealings are with an "in here"
This unbridged divide is cause for concern
In His infinite wisdom God sent us His Son
In a being that was anthropomorphic
To see and to touch and tell the Good News
With a voice that was more than angelic
Go to the Bible and learn from this man
The epitome of love and of grace
And never let go of that blessed hope
That someday we will see Him, face to face

2015

# It is Never Convenient

That the physical end of our fragile lives
Can creep up on us so unexpected
An intrusion, unwelcomed and insensitive
It violates all that's respected
The reaper can't seem to get enough of our living
Enjoys all the discord he imparts
He should know that our being is a lasting soul
Wrapped up in our spirits and our hearts
And although he will savor the confusion and havoc
His untimely actions will create
Be assured that our Savior has vanquished death
And our future will have a better fate
When Jesus was crucified, buried and mourned
The story didn't end in the grave
He arose to a new life which will never end
Hallelujah, be redeemed, let him save

2012

# Does My Life Have Meaning?

I might have been the apple of my mother's eye
But did it really matter?
I might be the love of a special someone
That makes her heart go pitter-patter
My children had an advocate that
Kept their living nurtured and secured
And persons I befriended
Shared a bonding that endured
But when all is said and done
Can these relations justify?
The maintenance of all my cells
Throughout these years until I die
Can I believe there is deeper intention?
A purpose for my being
For my touching and tasting that can be so good
For my smelling and hearing and seeing
I believe in a God that created these senses
In my person so that I could know
Of his other creatures that pass by my way
So that together we would grow
Into His body that is called His Church
Created solely for His pleasure
My worth is grounded when He declares
Me, to be a priceless treasure

2015

# Known by Our Hopes

Job, income security and good health
Independence and peaceful coexistence
These goals become the worldly means
By which we shape our lives
To be fulfilled
We worship wealth to empower
All these graces
Our hopes are firmly rooted in
The temporal and material
Awaken Lord our knowledge of your Spirit
Give us a passion
For the sense of the Divine
Teach us to know the Joy
Of saving grace
And the gift of righteousness
We never earned
Redirect our aims and hopes
To all that's Holy
May we learn more from our Saviour
Who sustains
And look beyond the here and now
To things eternal
To that Kingdom life with Christ
Our blessed hope

2000

# How Then Shall We Worship?

As ones created to do His will
We come before that Holy Presence
Are blinded by God's glorious light
And humbled by our minute essence
What can I do to give Him praise?
To celebrate this enthroned King
And who am I that He should care?
My weak attempts at worshiping

Be still and know this triune God
The father, spirit, sacrificed lamb
Bring only your best and with reverence bow down
Before the One known as the great I AM
Burst into songs of joyous praise
Join in harmony with all the redeemed
Shout the Amen, Jehovah reigns
Our worship is more than it may have seemed

2015

# The God of Individualism

We are unique, each person with a *god-likeness*
Created for a purpose in this worldly space
We primp and preen our image and our ego
To satisfy the yearnings that reside within
Our narcissistic slants ensure our needs are met

The center of my universe becomes just me
To maximize my pleasure and my power
Being careful that I don't offend my neighbor
In ways society deems to be incorrect
But guided by no higher rule or power

Flying solo in this world was not intended
We're programmed to participate in a whole
With other folks created for their purpose
Each working for the wellbeing of the unit
Described by God to be His Body

So set your sights on community endeavors
Desire the best for neighbor and for foe
And listen to the yearnings of the others
That long for relationships with meaning
A taste of what was intended at creation

2014

# Music

Music is the language of the angels
Its laws of harmony defined by God
Of tones and overtones and counter measures
Its cadence set by metronome and rod
Music evokes strong feelings in most people
Of patriotic power, pride and love
Its pathos reaches deeper than just verbiage
It draws one to a higher power above
God's love that's shared on earth between two lovers
Is oft' communicated in a song
The blending of soft notes with true endearment
Can make completely right the vilest wrong
And when collectively man comes before Him
In churches 'round the world, in every tongue
They laud, they praise, they magnify, they worship
With voices, organs, bells and even drum
When God made man according to His likeness
And breathed into his form a living soul
He gave to each the language of the angels
To harmonize with nature, their just goal
And so we sing with voices not yet perfect
A foretaste of the heaven that's yet to come
Where with the mighty throngs of angel voices
MUSIC will worship Father, Spirit, Son

1994

# Why I Believe

In orbits, hundreds of miles high
The astronauts can best observe
The heavenly precision which
Guides the galaxies
They conquer space at hundreds
Of miles per minute
In eerie solitude

At seven miles above the fields
Man's ordering powers are clearly evident
Yet details of each human endeavor
Cannot be seen
We speed at ten miles per minute
On man-made wings
And jets of power

I rush down sidewalks on my way
To business I deem right and urgent
Cognizant of the joy, sadness and pain
That's faced on others
I move at four miles per hour
On determined legs
Powered by muscular contraction

And after hours of tedious work each day
I lie beside my mate in bed
Reacting to her joyful charms and
Resting in her love
With little motion, but no haste
There's meeting of the bodies
And the minds

I can't believe that heavenly and human order,
That love and emotions of mankind
Are simply quirks of entropy and
Molecular vibrations
These wonders are expressions of
A master planner and
A present God

1987

# Aspen, Pine and Tamarack

Autumn in the Kootenay's
Provokes a most ostentatious display
Of spirited color
The pines stand firm
In their dark greens
Awaiting winter
While tamarack needles
Turn to brilliant yellows
Before their fall to earth
And aspen leaves are hued
In yellow and orange
To complement the scene
This kaleidoscope of color
Drapes itself upon the mountain slopes
In forms that seem to change
With every different vantage
I'm humbled by this beauty
That God deemed fit
To devise
For the pleasure of His people
Enjoy and give Him praise

2004

# Springtime

The warming of the air and earth
As solar rays dissolve the winter
Alerts one to the imminence
Of nature's metamorphic wonders
The birds sing forth with joyful glee
While busying themselves with nesting
With energies already used
To fly their airy marathon
The dormant seeds and frozen roots
By nature's stimuli are quickened
To transformations so diverse
The outcome, bounteous form and color
And lovers are the first to sense
These surging currents of new life
Added to their amorous bliss
Propels them to euphoric heights
And others dare not stand aloof
While all the world enjoys renewal
This season of new life and hope
Is prelude to real growth and harvest
Be thankful that the natural law
Allows for diverse constant change
Exploit these seasonal dynamics
To optimize your mode in springtime

1994

# Swallows In Springtime

Only fifty grams of biological might
That pump their wings with passion
To rise to heights for unknown purpose
Only to make an unpredicted lateral lurch
That seems so inconsistent with their flight
They glide for just a while before
The pumping of their wings begins anew
To raise them up to new heights
From which another lurch and glide begins

My view includes dozens of these crazed birds
That dance this frenzy of ecstatic bliss
For no obvious reason
It can't be just their route from A to B
I wonder whether it's their time for mating
But then again it might be just their praise
Their tribute to our God who made the seasons
Whose wings cannot be bound by reason
When sunshine warms our earth each springtime

2016

# Their Garden at Morning

As the long rays of morning sun
Burst over yonder trees to warm their garden
The dew drops on the herbs and grass
Seek refuge for another day

The birds dash here and there
Then perch to sing some morning praises
Appear to be in tune with the grand oneness
Of God's awesome and complex creation.

The gentle breezes of clean air
Flooded my lungs to full intoxication
Honing my senses to a level of awareness
That confirmed within, a joy to be alive

And then an autumn leaf came wafting by my table
A lesson that all life is for a season
Urging us to vitalize each daily moment
As we come to learn our work within His garden

1998

# Morning Musings

I sit amongst our garden life
The trees, the shrubs, the grass
With swallows darting here and there
All part of nature's mass
They play their part in earthy worship
Their roles can be debated
But come each year, the play goes on
To a script that was divinely created
And who am I? God's resident gardener
Who makes and maintains these plots
Water their roots from underground lines
And dares to grow some in pots
Is all of this living some random occurrence?
We've exploited to bring us pleasure
Or are they part of a plan that is hidden from man
That tells of a Holy endeavor
I can believe in an Almighty Power
Who designed and created the physical
By processes revealed to us new everyday
Learned from our deduction and analytical
God's creation we're told was very, very good
But man has corrupted this space
When Christ will return He'll make everything new
And we will behold Him, face to face

2015

# The Matter that Really Matters

Each being has a substance that is physical
We're made up of many diverse cells
Which in turn are made of molecules
Which in turn are made of atoms
Which in turn are made of fundamental particles
Whose building blocks have yet to be revealed
This physical matter is structured by basic laws
Into useful bits that make up what we see and feel

This substance of the material world
Is common to both the living and the inanimate
The molecules and electrons that define each person
Have probably had a role in previous expressions
And though our material self has great importance
These configurations are transient and doomed
Our substance will return to dusty matter
Soon after what's vital to our being is gone

Each being has another reality that is spiritual
Whose substance has eluded our best inquiry
So life was superimposed upon our physical matter
When at creation's moment, God breathed His breath on man
Combining flesh and spirit into a union
That defines a being with some likeness of his God
We humans breathe, communicate and love
By complex processes known only to the Creator

The Bible teaches that our spiritual substance
Has a lasting reality that will live forever
And when our bodies die and degrade to dust
Our true being lives on in some spiritual realm
Awaiting that time when Christ returns to earth

To recreate His universe into a perfect space
Where our real matter will play a strategic role
In His Kingdom that will have no end

2012

# The Power of Love

Love
When impounded within
Can't possibly fulfill its
Intended
Meaning

Love
When freely shared
Can obviate
All pains
And fears

Love
Found in a Holy God
Can transform
Me into
His likeness

2002

# It's Been Some Years

It's been some years since chaos struck
Terrorizing the unsuspected
The trickle-down of bad effects
Has been greater than was first predicted
Financial loss could reach a few trillions
When all has been added and done
And the culprits alleged to have planned the deed
Are out there and still on the run
Military might was mustered, security heightened
As we strove to respond and cope
But for many the fears will go on for years
As we search for some reasons to hope
Not enough has been made of the underlying grievance
That prompted the terrorists to strike
If we don't try to learn, and show little concern
We'll be doomed by the scorn of dislike
How should the mightiest nation on earth
Review its political stance?
Should the cards be reshuffled, show more equity
As we do our international dance?
It's a time for forgiveness, feeding enemies
By a nation that is Christian in name
But the powers of evil so strongly entrenched
Will arrogantly resist, for shame

2010

# DNA, RNA, Proteins and Enzymes

Each cell in our body is programmed from the start
To manufacture the proteins of each tissue
These catalytic and structural building blocks
Define the superstructure upon which our lives are draped
How fifty trillion of them get their duty mostly right
Has puzzled those that wonder at this spectacle
But now we know that the master code is embedded in DNA
That meter long molecule squished into each cell nucleus
And the triplet sequence of the A, T, C, G basic letters
Determines which amino acid is linked next
Into threads of protein stuff that is folded up for function
So that their electronic surface can do the rest
All these biochemical reactions take place in just plain water
Albeit at some very high concentration
Most human cells can duplicate in the space of just one day
To make a clone and mitotically divide
It takes almost fifty such divisions to produce one adult person
Just from that first uniquely fertilized cell
And most of these divisions take place within a mother
Before the newborn sees the light of day
I do not have the faith to believe these astounding processes
Just happened over time by random chance
It was into this physical object of metabolic wonder
That God breathed His breath to complete His creatures

2016

# Cancer

A myriad of anabolic processes
Each in its turn,
Sequentially, and with precision
Producing two of every kind
Then with an order most astounding
The likes repel
Creating two, from just the one
Such is the process
Whereby cells, the stuff of life,
Are known to grow and reproduce
This scheme in all its beauty
When controlled
Is vital and life giving
Human forms stem from units
Thus mitotically divided and
Functioning together in arrays
Toward a common end
This scheme maintains
A steady flow of transient parts
Essential for good health
And when our flesh is bruised
It leaps forth from its dormancy
To repair damaged tissue
And to heal the hurt
And yet this very process
So essential
For our life
Our growth
Our health
And our healing
At times becomes uncoupled
From its intended role
Resulting in an uncontrolled growth

Of inconspicuous cells
Each adding to a mass of
Undesired tissue
Such a malignant zone can
Sap the body of its needed nurture
Obstruct the normal functions of the organs
And bring man to
A premature and painful death
Can a more hideous crime be found
Than using Nature's perfect scheme
Designed for life
To promote death?

1979

# A Poet's Creed

## ON DEATH

Its tragic blow stalks through this mortal world
Respecting neither race, nor class, nor age
Intent to end each God-created life
And bring a hell to each, and those who're left.
What is this hideous force that rears its ugly head?
Amidst the unsuspecting tranquil of a day
And dashes man's attempts at peaceful life
Leaving suffering, pain and utter disarray
Did some creator wishing to conserve
Simply devise a balance force?
Or is our pain merely inconsequence
As matter slides its thermodynamic course?

The Galilean taught a perfect plan
How God in His omnipotence and love
Created man, according to His likeness
As keeper of the earth in which he moved
And breathed into these designated stewards
By process we may never comprehend
His Spirit, whereby each could know his Maker
To share His paradise that knows no end.
Man, thus, became the paramount of creation
And capable of fellowship with God
His life an endless, joyous orchestration
Of peace and love and everything that's good.

Onto this perfect scene an evil spirit
Antithesis to God and all He'd made
Crept with disguise and calculated malice
Intent to nullify the bliss they had,
Thus man became beguiled by the Devil

Believing his life-station incomplete
He lusted for the knowledge of his Maker
Disrupting their relationship so sweet
But gained through his allegiance to the other
The wages he so willingly *provideth*
Of pain and fear and constant discontent
A broken body rushing on to DEATH.


## ON LIFE

Alas, alas, what hope is there for man
This creature to be pitied all his days
Created for communion with his Maker
Found wallowing in such various sinful ways.
And yet, the love of God for his created
Drove him to send his Son in manlike form
To live and walk amongst his fallen stewards
To teach them of the call for which they're born.
He tried to reawaken in their bosoms
His spirit deadened by their constant sin
And told them of a reconciliation,
Of fellowship 'tween men and God, again.

Many listened to the message of His teachings
But few would follow in the path He trod
And in the end the universe did tremble
As man crucified the VERY SON OF GOD.
His grave became the scene of mighty battle
Of all that ever raged, the most profound
He arose the victor over sin and Satan
Death's deepest vaults could never keep Him bound.
The curse of death was conquered by this Savior
"Man's grave no longer holds its ugly sting"

For though we die, a blessed hope is offered
Of life eternal, with this Christ, the King.

And still today man searches for a meaning
To life and death, to joy and peace and pain
His willful, sinful nature ever present
A burden from his birth to last refrain.
So shout the GOOD NEWS to each burdened creature
That God is love and dearly loves each one
Christ Jesus conquered death and offers new life
Eternal with the Father and the Son.
If we would dare to reach out to this Savior
In faith, God's loving spirit would rush in
To cleanse our broken forms with His forgiveness
Restoring perfect fellowship again.

Then life would take on meaning and direction
An integer within God's cosmic plan
A witness to His great redeeming power
A balm to soothe the hurts in fellow man.
His forgiveness would help us be forgiving
His love would teach us how to love
Our life on earth would be just the beginning
To life eternal to be shared above.
And although these bodies die, scarred by corruption
Whether violent, painful, slow, or premature
We can know beyond the grave is resurrection
In God's Kingdom that will evermore endure.

1970

# Transitions

When circumstances rear their ugly heads
When life seems dark and full of dire foreboding
When all one's hopes and dreams appear to shatter
Beneath the weight of fear that's overloading

How can the light of peace and love break in?
Dispel despair and gloom within our souls
Can one believe that Christ has conquered death?
When ears are only filled with deathbed tolls

Rejoice, His plan for man has been accomplished
Resurrection guarantees eternal life
And for those who claim His promise of salvation
They will pass into His presence, free from strife

2012

# What Lies Beyond?

What lies beyond this life we live?
And often come to love
Can it be true that God has made?
A home in realms above
The Bible teaches of a place
Beyond this life, called Glory
That we will live eternally
Is a most provocative story
But the here and now is tangible
We can touch and see and hear
And the great beyond is veiled from sight
Unknowns are things that we fear
Why should we devote our energies?
To details beyond the physical
Our scientific knowledge base
Defines quite well the factual
We can regulate our daily lives
So as to maximize our pleasure
Store up nest eggs for future meals
Secure in our own earthly treasure
But as our lives begin to ebb
And our control begins to fray
We can end up spending all of the bank
Just to have one extra day
When will we learn that God has prepared?
An eternal city for his own
Those who will trust in His perfect plan
His citizens robed in righteous gown
The good things and times of our earthly sojourn
Are foretaste of the heaven that waits
But to be going home should arouse deep hopes
Even when we don't know times and dates
So live your life to the fullest, take time to love

Those who God brings into your story
Always look to that goal, with heart, mind and soul
As you make your way home to glory

1992

# Holistic Philosophy

When I dwell on deeper meanings for my life
There are two tracks of revelation that are known
The first is from the wonders of this world
The diverse forms of matter and the stone
How and when the billion galaxies were hurled
Into a void that shocks our sense of vastness
And why the rugged mountains were upheaved
Creating superficial beauty that seems endless
Then adding to these puzzles in our thinking
Is the fact that I can muse and analyze
Attempt to find a oneness in creation
The reason for my being and the skies
The second track for learning of one's purpose
Are the words for life that long ago were spoken
By the Christ who came to earth as God incarnate
Made a way for restoration of we broken
Through His exemplary life and teachings
We learn lives were created for His plan
To shine His light of love to those around us
And to heal the hurts of every fellowman
When our scientific knowledge of the physical
Is melded to the message in God's word
We can know a wholeness to our living
Relaxing in the wisdom of Our Lord

2016

# A Prayer

Lord Jesus our Messiah
I bow before the majesty
Of your created wonders
The precision with which
The heavens and earth
Continue on their temporal courses
The harmonic wholeness
Seen all around me
In the flora and fauna

I marvel in knowing
That your redemptive blood
That flowed at Calvary
Creates new life in even me
Fill me with your Spirit and love
And graft me deep within
The fullness of your cosmic plan
So that the witness of my life
Will show your love
And be divinely blessed

AMEN

# ABOUT THE AUTHOR

J. Donald Chapman was born in Estevan, Saskatchewan, Canada, the son of a grocer who taught him much about stacking shelves, checking out groceries, driving the delivery truck and working on the business books. It could be said that this apprenticeship was as great a part of his education as his formal schooling. It is unfortunate that most kids today never get such a chance. His university training was in engineering physics, radiation physics and biophysics and was not a path that he predetermined. Doors were opened by making the required grades and accepting scholarships. He was mentored and trained during his university years by four icons of the radiation research field; in radiation physics (Doug Cormack), radiation chemistry (Ged Adams), cell biology and biophysics (Ernest Pollard) and charged-particle radiotherapy (Cornelius Tobias). His career has been blessed with success in obtaining peer-reviewed grants, mentoring several brilliant graduate students and medical residents, serving on several editorial boards and receiving six international research awards. Much of his research is summarized in the medical physics textbook, "Radiotherapy Treatment Planning – Linear/ Quadratic Radiobiology" that was published in 2015 by CRC Press.

Don was raised in a Christian family with five other kids, was taken to Sunday School every Sunday, doted over by a loving mother and nurtured by the greater family of aunts, uncles and grandfather. He was supported during his university years by participation in functions of Inter-Varsity Christian Fellowship. It can be said that he was as diligent in seeking understanding about matters of his faith as about his science. From graduate school days, he began writing his musings on specific themes of nature and faith in poetry of free verse and rhyme. This became his personal habit for fixing his current thoughts in words that others would understand. So words and language were an important tool for both his development as a scientist and as a mature Christian. Some poems were previously published in the volume, FAITH IN WORDS – A POET'S CREED, Durango Publishing of Penticton, BC. That compilation was designed mainly for family and friends and included several poems that had been written for family reunions and personal events. This current volume has been compiled for those who struggle with questions relating to the meaning to their lives and if we really matter. Popular science today teaches that we humans are the end product of an evolution of matter that was exploded some 14 billion years ago into the cosmic space we can see today with sophisticated observatories. Now much of what modern science is observing and describing is undoubtedly true but the Christian faith teaches that the physical also has an important spiritual meaning. So while there has developed a fault-line between science and faith over the past hundred or so years, both approaches strive to seek the truth about physical reality and the meaning of human life. The author believes that these are complimentary revelations that should attempt to learn from each other instead of trying to outdo the other. It should be apparent that this author does not have enough faith to be an atheist and certainly is still searching for true answers to many questions.

Printed in the United States
By Bookmasters